For Sons and Grandsons

Gardenia T. Bulluck, ACS., M.S., Ed.S., Ph.D. Min

Foreword Pastor R. L. Tillery, Sr.

Edited 2025

First Print Copyright © 2022

All rights reserved. No part of this book may be reproduced, stored, or transmitted by any means—whether auditory, graphic, mechanical, or electronic—without the written permission of the author.

The views expressed in this work are solely those of the author or contributors and do not necessarily reflect the views of the publisher, and the publisher hereby disclaims any responsibility for them.

Scripture is taken from The Holy Bible, Amplified (AMP), International Version® NIV® Copyright © 1973 1978 1984 2011 by Biblica, Inc. TM. Online English Standard Version (ESV) 2022 and New King James Version (NKJV) Copyright © 1982 by Thomas Nelson. Used by permission.

All rights reserved.

ISBN:978-1-7330473-5-7

DEDICATION

To all Sons and Grandsons Across this World

What we all do in these bodies impacts our lives and the lives of others. Therefore, I wish you well in your body, mind, and spirit. Seek Him in the season of NOW.

To my Miracle-birthed Grandsons

One day, our physical bodies will no longer reside here on earth. I hope your impact will leave a legacy of love inspired by God's power and Truth for generational blessings.

To Nephews and Great-Nephews

As I write this book, God called Aaron to his heavenly home. We are grateful for the five years that God allowed him to laugh, live, and make our lives brighter. Dedicating this work is one way to celebrate each of you. I love you.

I did not give birth to you, but my love for you is of God and strong. God has given you as an instrument to lead your children. Lead by faith and love for Him. You are a blessing!

To My Brothers

May God continue strengthening your roles as husbands, fathers, grandfathers, and mentors. Max and Roderick, how richly blessed I am by you.

To My Loving and Supportive Husband

My love for you is stronger than ever. I love you so much. I am so blessed every day that God gives us. Always, my lover and friend. God made you just for me.

CONTENTS

	Acknowledgments	i
	Foreword – Rev. Dr. R. L. Tillery	ii
1	From Your Proverbial Mom	Pg 1
2	Are You a Barrier to My Soul or…	Pg 7
3	Your Peace is not Dependent Upon…	Pg 16
4	Marriage versus Parenthood	Pg 26
5	Understanding Your Spirit Man	Pg 31
6	The Gift is More than the Pain	Pg 36
7	My Dear	Pg 42
8	How Do You Break Through?	Pg 46
9	When You Look Like Your Daddy	Pg 52
10	Building	Pg 60
11	Wisdom is More Than Knowledge	Pg 65
12	Bittersweet	Pg 77
	Why Sons & Grandsons?	Pg 83
	About the Author	Pg 87

For Sons and Grandsons - The Legacy You Deserve

ACKNOWLEDGMENTS

To my family, who continues to support and encourage me

I am not flawless, but you capture the pictures of love that I wish to leave behind. Thank you for inspiring me in so many ways. Thank you for believing in what God has entrusted to me – a legacy of love.

With love,
Nana

Foreword

In Genesis Chapter 4, verse 9, God asks a powerful question. He asks Cain where is thy brother? Cain responds by saying, "I know not." However, Cain did not stop at that simple, direct statement. Instead, Cain asks a poignant question. He asks, "Am I my brother's keeper?" In many circles, people have pondered the question of whether one has a responsibility towards another. Am I truly responsible for "keeping my brother?" Unequivocally, the answer is yes. As a man of God, a child of God, a servant of God, a citizen of heaven, and a recipient of sound mentoring from a previous generation, I am responsible for being my brother's keeper. If I serve as my brother's keeper, I will not commit violence against my brother. If I am my brother's keeper, I will not physically, emotionally, financially, socially, or spiritually harm my brother. If I were my brother's keeper, I would love my brother and seek ways to build him up. I will share with him if I am my brother's keeper, so he grows. If I were my brother's keeper, I would invest in him.

Who is my brother? My natural DNA does not define my brother. My brother is every son, every grandson, every uncle, every brother, every father, and every grandfather.

Growing up as the youngest male child was challenging. I looked to "the village" to show me how to be a man. My father, William, was my role model. I strived to be like my natural daddy with every fiber of my being. I looked to my uncle, Haywood, for guidance as well. These two men taught me how to be a man. They taught me the value of family. They taught me how to love God. I honor my eldest brother Bernard because he showed me how to care for my family. He exemplified how to be an entrepreneur and entertainer, but most importantly, he emphasized that the focus must be on caring for family, as given by God. I honor my brother Max because he exemplifies that we are always family and family sticks together. I honor my sons, Jevon, Michael, and Roderick Jr. My sons make me a better father. I am honored to be their father. I am honored to be an example for them so they can be an example for their children. I honor my grandsons, Jeremiah, Frederick, Jahte'z, Jadyne, Michael Jr., Aaron Ayden, Theopolis, Logan, and Ashton. These grandsons have allowed me to love them and model how to be a man. I honor every man in my life: from my grandfather to my nephews, to my pastors, to my friends, who have poured into my life to help me become a good son or grandson.

Rev. Dr. Gardenia T. Bulluck authored *"For Sons and Grandsons"* to provide guidance and insight for future generations. Each generation is responsible for teaching the next about the family while simultaneously inspiring them to build on a sure foundation and create greatness. I had the opportunity to know how great my ancestors were because individuals shared the value of family. Rev. Bulluck has shared "Spiritual Nuggets" that will have positive life implications. This book dives into a conversation with *Sons and Grandsons* with the hope of building up our young men. The book reminds our young men where to find their peace, how to walk at their own pace, and how to lead as a marriage partner and a father. Readers of this book will be elated to learn how to look like our daddy. It is refreshing to know that regardless of who our natural father is, we should all strive to look like our heavenly father.

I have mentioned several men who shaped and provided wisdom in my life. I am grateful for every male figure in my life. However, I want to recognize the females who have been instrumental in my life. I am thankful for my grandmothers (Pearl and Sallie), who were firm and loving, and set the foundation for our family. I am grateful for my mothers (Vernell and Pearl), who provided life, acceptance, lessons, love, and unmatched protection. I am thankful for Sandy and Gardenia showing me how brothers and sisters can love each other from the depths of our souls. I am grateful for my wife, Renee, whom God designed just for me. I am thankful for my daughters, Tisha and Shakessha, whom I love wholeheartedly and will always be daddy's girls. I am grateful for my amazing granddaughters (Keonte, Brittany, and Kayla). I am thankful for my daughters-in-law (Marnisha and Laneesha), whom my sons love and cherish. I am grateful for our Aunts (Elaine and Tine), who have loved us beyond measure. I am thankful for two amazing nieces (Melissa and Kendra) who exemplify the meaning of Godly Women. I honor these women for how they have poured into and cherished the men. I honor these women for never tearing down our men but loving us in our imperfections while standing with us as we become what God created us to be.

Many women find themselves raising young men. I want to share that you can raise a young man, but the male child cannot be your man. Take the lessons in this book to share with your sons and grandsons. Take the "Spiritual Nuggets" and allow yourself, as the reader, to spark dialogue. Allow the book to serve as a catalyst to foster generational blessings.

"For Sons and Grandsons" is designed to speak positivity over our young men. The book is designed to move young men to be the absolute best. The lessons shared in this book are grounded and rooted in love. The book is designed to leave a legacy for the author and serve as inspiration for the reader.

The question has been asked, "Am I my brother's keeper?" Yes, I am!

Rev. Dr. Roderick L. Tillery, Sr., Pastor

For Sons and Grandsons - The Legacy You Deserve

"The Legacy You Build Is Yours. Your Legacy Matters! Own It Outright!"

The Author [Self]

Chapter 1

FROM YOUR PROVERBIAL MOM
Letter Number Twenty-three

Another year and James returned to his Mom's home, where he first learned his life values.

A great deal had happened during the pandemic. The children were being homeschooled. Laura was working from home while he worked 12-hour days with little time off. These life-changing events were not much different from those experienced by other people they knew. Throughout these times, James stayed in contact with his Mom through telephone conversations. This week off would give him a chance to check on Mom physically. He could already taste his *Proverbial Mom's* cornbread, greens, and candied yams.

James was grateful for Mom's church family, who had provided an additional support system during the pandemic. Even though James and Mom could FaceTime each other, it was different from those close-up hugs. He knew that once he was there, her eyes would tell him all he needed to know – that she was well.

He hoped the list of house chores would remain simple, consisting of small tasks, even after the pandemic, because their timely talks had always meant the most. Their talks on past trips were always varied, covering topics like his Dad, job, family, college days, and world events. Like all the other trips, he looked forward to these good talks and great eating. The only thing to regret about the past trips is having to leave.

When James arrived, Mom's eyes told him she was well, and joy filled her face to see him. After a few days, it was time to prepare for his return.

The night before James was to leave, he fell asleep in the den watching TV. Mom dared not awake him; she watched him snore aloud with the "lungs of his father." She smiled. She thought, "When you were seven years old, when you and Dad fell asleep like this, I would wake you both. I could pick you up, carry you, and gently lay you in bed. Not now, my son. Now, you can pick Mom up." She paused to thank God for this moment and for how He was keeping James. James will leave for home in a few hours – physically – yet always in her heart. It was time to write letter #23. Mom returned to her room, sat at her desk, and began the letter.

True to form, upon his return home, James anxiously took the letter from his suitcase. This time, a folded, wrinkled paper was inside the envelope. James began to read before opening the folded, wrinkled paper inside.

My Dear Son,

I continue to pray for you, seeking wisdom and understanding from God. God is Truth, and Truth is everlasting. The Father of righteousness sees you. He is not slack in His knowledge. He knows the matter of every soul, every cause and effect. No man goes unpunished.

I caution you as the Word says, "Do not rejoice when an evil man falls. The same Lord is at hand. If you faint in the day of adversity, your strength is small. When you help another see the error of their ways, you increase knowledge and build wisdom, Proverbs 24:17-18."

As you live, you will see stranger things, and your heart will bleed over perverse things. The increase of unfaithful men will perhaps startle you. Many will prefer to hurt people experiencing poverty. Because of power and love for money, their gluttony is like that of a drunkard.

However, my son, you must desire the *honey of life* because it is good. It is sweet to your taste. Your hope will not be cut off because the Lord continually provides for your needs. He fills the lives of those who love him with precious and pleasant riches that are beyond the comforts of this life.

Remember, the Lord will restore your soul and lead you by still waters that will not overtake you. According to Isaiah 43:2 AMP, When you pass through the waters, he will be with you. The rivers will not overwhelm you. Even when you walk through the fire, you will not be scorched; the flame will not burn you. God has promised that the righteous will prevail. Yes, a man who walks in the counsel of the Almighty and does not sit in the seat of the scornful is blessed.

The power given by mere men through fear is fleeting and unstable. They make travel dangerous in every way. They speak falsehoods. Their foundation is built on sand. They take counsel among weak men and walk in darkness. On the other hand, your help comes from the Lord to give strength. The power provided by the Lord lifts the light of the soul; it puts gladness in your heart. It produces in the summer, fall, winter, and spring seasons.

Remember, the earth is the Lord's and all its fullness; the world and those who dwell in it (Psalm 24:1). For those who trust in the Lord, one may walk through the valley of the shadow of death; you do not need to fear because the Lord is with you.

Understand that no man can go in his own strength. He does not breathe on his own. It is the Lord who knows the number of his days. It is God who allows all to spend their days on this earth. It is God who is the judge of those days.

Therefore, my son, fulfill your days to the honor of his glory, and he will direct your path. Your steps must be according to this will and way.

Anger is part of living; so are sadness and love. However, be quick to listen, slow to speak, and slow to anger (James 1:9). Learn the songs of praise that honor the Lord. This will soothe your spirit. You can count on God's love that overshadows any other. His love is timeless; His grace is sufficient even in unpleasantness.

God's mercy is new every day. He has established a plan that no man can foil. Yes, he plans to help you prosper. Pray to the Lord for it, because if it prospers, you too will prosper (Jeremiah 29:7). Any load or burden does not weigh down his arms. His hand is over all of humanity. He measures right from wrong, which cannot be changed.

Remember the poem you recited at age twelve for your school play – I kept it all these years. I am now returning it to its rightful owner."

"Invictus" by Henley (public domain)
Out of the night that covers me,
Black as the pit from pole to pole,
I thank whatever gods may be
For my unconquerable soul.
In the fell clutch of circumstance
I have not winced nor cried aloud.

Under the bludgeonings of chance
My head is bloody but unbowed.
Beyond this place of wrath and tears
Looms but the Horror of the shade,
And yet the menace of the years.
Finds and shall find me unafraid.
It matters not how strait the gate,
How charged with punishments the scroll,
I am the master of my fate,
I am the captain of my soul.

You must pray to be faithful to Him. Stand on that faith, my son, who has empowered you for this journey. This, my son, is *A nugget for life's journey – your legacy that I wish for you..*

Lovingly,
Your Proverbial Mom

Chapter 2

How Do You See Yourself?

ARE YOU A BARRIER TO MY SOUL OR A MOVEMENT TOWARD MY DESTINY?

"Are you a barrier to my soul or a movement toward my destiny?" Yes, that is the question. How do you fit into my life? Where does that person fit in your life? Do you add to my value? Do you subtract in ways that are counterproductive to my potential? After all, God wonderfully created me.

Picture this! I recall the day my oldest grandson came home crying because he felt he didn't have any friends. Friends? I could not ignore his pain, yet at the same time, I felt that anyone who knew his heart and the kind of person he was would be blessed by his friendship. At that time, he was only seven years old, but he knew enough about life to understand that friends were essential to him. A decade later, as a young man, he learned the difference between associates and friends. His idea about associates and friendships has certainly matured. How do I know this?

One Saturday morning, while we were having breakfast together, he spoke convincingly about how he viewed his choices regarding friendship and associates, particularly in relation to his life goals. I was ecstatic! I immediately left the room and returned with one of my prayer journals in hand. I opened the journal and began to read. The words that were coming from my mouth were from a prayer. These are the words I spoke to him more than ten years ago when he was visibly upset. We laughed out loud at how God had answered that prayer. My grandson was carefully choosing relationships based on the words spoken over him—"Dear God, Give him relationships with those assigned and according to Your plan for his life.

In that prayer, my grandson (although young at the time) agreed as I prayed over him. We prayed for people of good character and for the disentanglement of companionships that were not for God. In that prayer, we asked God for wisdom in forming and choosing friendships, both now and in the future. I remember that night, I wrote these questions in that journal regarding his relationships: *"Is that person of good character? Will that person make you smile or cry more? Will that person support your goals or hurt your chances of moving forward?"*

In conversations throughout his growing years, these were the questions I would ask him as he pondered relationships and identified those he would categorize as friends or associates. That Saturday morning, the words out of his mouth spoke of God's protection.

Yes, more than twenty years have passed, and we continue to ask and thank God for surrounding him with relationships to move him toward his destiny. Why? This is because it is for living an abundant life.

Standing on Fertile Ground: Reasons for Celebration and Calibration

In Isaiah 55:1 NIV, you will find these words, *"Come, all you who are thirsty; come to the waters; and you who have no money, come, buy and eat!"*

It further asks, "*Why do you spend money for what is not bread and your wages for what does not satisfy?*"

What does God mean by that? God's warning is not to waste your time, money, and energy on foolish companionships and things that are unworthy of your talents and the gifts He has given to you. God has a plan for you. Jeremiah 29:11 NIV says, **"For I know the plans I have for you," declares the Lord, "plans to prosper you and not to harm you, plans to give you hope and a future."** So, what must those friendships look like? The type of friendships that you need in life are those who will help you move toward those plans. Those friends understand what kind of bread one must seek - *the everlasting bread of life that feeds the soul and spirit.* God's friends want you to have an abundant life. This means you will not thirst after unrighteousness, but your ways and thoughts will come from Him. He desires and will direct you to the resources, including relationships, that He has provided for you on the earth until eternity. That is why Isaiah could say, "Everyone who thirsts, come to the waters; and you who have no money, come, buy grain and eat." Those friends exist to pray for you in desert storms.

Whom Should I Leave Behind?

What ties do you need to break when it comes to relationships? Think about it. If one does not understand that *the bread of life is more than the riches of this world,* should that person control one's ways and thoughts? Can you prosper in relationships that do not honor the glory of God? Are you able to lead people to higher ground if the Father does not protect you?

As youngsters, you may not have understood that. But as you mature in Christ, you can be confident in the Lord's willingness to guide you in such matters. Seek God and ask Him, *"Are those in my life supposed to be here in this season?"*

Have you considered that there might be a reason you continue to get involved with certain types of people? Could there be generational curses attached to you? Ask the Lord? *"Has someone spoken into my life or against me, and I am not aware of it?"*

These are very good reasons for praying and seeking the righteousness and guidance of the Father, for He can help you in detachments. He can help you form meaningful relationships that make a positive difference in your life.

What of those Entanglements?

God's kingdom people are at odds with the enemy of God; His enemy's name is Satan. So, you might also ask, *"Do I really need to be aware of people who are barriers to my soul? Do I really need to be aware of relationships that do not move me toward my destiny?"* The answer is clear in the Word of God. Ephesians 6:11-15 NIV, *"Put on the whole armor of*

God so that you can take your stand against the devil's schemes. For our struggle is not against flesh and blood, but against the rulers, against the authorities, against the powers of this dark world and against the spiritual forces of evil in the heavenly realms. Therefore, put on the whole armor of God, so that when the day of evil comes, you may be able to stand your ground and, after you have done everything, stand. Stand firm then, with the belt of truth buckled around your waist, with the breastplate of righteousness in place, and with your feet fitted with the readiness that comes from the gospel of peace.

You, as God's kingdom inheritance, have the Holy Father for your victory. 1 John 4:4 states, "You, dear children, are from God and have overcome them because the one (God) who is in you is greater than the one (Satan) who is in the world."

How Do I Fight? How Will My Friends Fight?

First, you have 'The Word of Truth.' Engage with the Word daily. Guard your heart with the Word of God. Speak and encourage yourself. Feel free to acknowledge the pain in your circumstances, but do not live in fear. God's people are not meant to decrease but increase in wisdom. The Spirit of Truth is available to lead and comfort you (the Holy Spirit).

Second, weaponize yourself with the power of prayer. A strong prayer life is essential as a defensive strategy. All of your answers are in Him who created you. He knows what your needs are and understands the desires of your heart. Pray the will of God for yourself and your companionship. Pray for the victory that you have been promised, and it is yours.

Third, true companionship is from Him; the three are one: God the Father, Christ Jesus, and the Holy Spirit. They are the revealer as One. Christ had earthly companions, such as Peter, John, and James. He understands the value of real, genuine friendships. The people who accompanied Christ were not perfect, but they shared a like-minded faith, honor, and commitment to God. God chose men of valor for this purpose. He continues to do so today. Surround yourself with people who are equally passionate about the kingdom of God and are willing to fight the good fight.

Christ Jesus is always willing to be the nearest companion. He is ever-present. He is dedicated to helping you move toward your purpose and your friends toward theirs.

Conclusion – Final Nuggets

As a nugget, my simple advice to sons and grandsons continues to be, *"If someone is not there to move you toward your destiny, you must avoid that company at all costs. Such is the kingdom. Do not entangle yourself with women or men who do not have your best interest at heart. Excuse yourself from their company. Such people will weave you into webs of deception and confusion."* According to 1 Corinthians 10:13 ESV, "No temptation has overtaken you that is not common to man. God is faithful, and he will not let you be tempted beyond your ability, but with a temptation, he will also provide a way of escape, that you may be able to endure it." God never tempts people. Only Satan tempts.

God has already spoken into your destiny. He knew you before you were formed in the belly of your mother and knows all your thoughts (Jeremiah 1:5; Psalm 139:1-18). But everyone has been given freewill.

It pleased the Father when my grandsons shared with me that their daily affirmation is, *"For I know the plans I have for you, declares the Lord, plans for your welfare and not for evil, to give you a future and a hope. Then you will call upon me and come and pray to me, and I will hear you. You will seek me and find me, when you seek me with all your heart,"* Jeremiah 29:11-13 ESV. Therefore, our job as a family is to encourage and support them as the Father leads them into their destiny.

Finally, to all sons and grandsons everywhere, I share these scriptural verses to remind you that God has established a way to remove barriers, including even ungodly relationships, as He has promised.

Blessed is the man who walks not in the counsel of the wicked, nor stands in the way of sinners, nor sits in the seat of scoffers; but his delight is in the law of the Lord, and on his law, he meditates day and night.

He is like a tree planted by streams of water that yields its fruit in its season, and its leaf does not wither. In all that he does, he prospers.
Psalms 1:1-3 NKJV

Prosper in the way of the Lord, sons and grandsons.

Chapter 3

Smiles are precious and should be valued, especially when they are freely given with love. Thank you, MJ.

YOUR PEACE IS NOT DEPENDENT UPON SOMEONE ELSE

Your peace is not dependent upon someone else's. Instead, peace is dependent upon how you respond to the situation. Genuine peace means that you will not let circumstances *get* to you.

In life, you will have troubles. The Bible tells us that the days of a man, born of a woman, are short and filled with struggles/troubles (Job 14:1). Your response to a crisis can bring about peace, or it can bring worry.

The peace that surpasses your human understanding is not from another human being; instead, it must come from God.

Handling the Crisis – the Storm

What is the crisis? When the storms in your life rage, what will be **your response in the storm?** Will you take flight *as an eagle* or perch *like a crow*? What of the eagle? I am glad you want to know.

The eagle has an eye capable of seeing miles away. Isaiah 40:31 NIV compares those who operate as eagles as this… *"but those who hope in the Lord will renew their strength. They will soar on wings like eagles; they will run and not grow weary; they will walk and not be faint."*

An eagle flies **above the storms,** where the eagle can be at peace. While flying, when an eagle gets tired (while in flight), it uses the wind to glide so that it is at rest during its flight. To rest as an eagle, my son, means you will **relax in Christ** in life's journey. You must be dependent upon His strength that is operating in you.

In nature, storms are violent because of atmospheric disturbances. Pressure, clouds, strong winds, lightning, and thunder characterize these weather phenomena. Life consists of raging storms characterized by stress, disasters, and hardships. Finding peace amid storms requires placing your faith and hope in God. No human and another god (materialistic or otherwise) can bring you peace that surpasses (goes beyond) your human understanding amid a storm or crisis in your life. This peace is not like the world gives; it is a type of peace that only the Heavenly Father can provide. How is it that a person can stand firm when hell is breaking loose in their life? How is it that a mother can come out of her prayer closet and declare, "God got this!" How is it that a trodden-down father can lift his hands in church and cry out, "I know He will fix it!" What is it that makes a person in a crisis say, "It is still well."

These are examples of eagles who move among us. These are examples of people who have had *eagle experiences* and know what it is to have peace that surpasses human understanding. And yes, it is available to anyone who will trust Him.

On the other hand, the crow is a different bird. It has humanistic behaviors, too. It has some good traits, but this bird tends to be noisy.

It squawks loudly. Its voice is distinctive from others because of its noise. They love to mourn their circumstances. They want a company of mourners. Its behaviors are very observable as a mourning bird among other crows. Yet, they, too, are clever, thoughtful, and proven problem solvers. However, scientists have observed these birds under various circumstances and found that they hold grudges, unlike eagles.

Decision-time – Your Choice

So, how will you operate in times of storms? Will you be like an eagle and ask God to help you fly above the storm to reach an attitude where you can glide and know that He is operating as the wind beneath your wings? How will peace in your life be defined? As a soaring eagle or a perched crow? How can you obtain harmony in your circumstances? What does peace look like in a crisis?

Consider the directives given by Jesus in Matthew 5 concerning the attitudes of people. In this sermon, Jesus defines the behaviors of those who are at peace on earth and will obtain everlasting peace. Jesus called such people who operate under such conditions "blessed." Because he is there to aid them.

Matthew 5:2-11 ESV

And he opened his mouth and taught them, saying:

³ "Blessed are the poor in spirit, for theirs is the kingdom of heaven.

⁴ "Blessed are those who mourn, for they shall be comforted.

⁵ "Blessed are the meek, for they shall inherit the earth.

⁶ "Blessed are those who hunger and thirst for righteousness, for they shall be satisfied.

⁷ "Blessed are the merciful, for they shall receive mercy.

⁸ "Blessed are the pure in heart, for they shall see God.

⁹ "Blessed are the peacemakers, for they shall be called sons of God.

¹⁰ "Blessed are those who are persecuted for righteousness' sake, for theirs is the kingdom of heaven.

¹¹ "Blessed are you when others revile you and persecute you and utter all kinds of evil against you falsely on my account. ¹² Rejoice and be glad, for your reward is great in heaven, for so they persecuted the prophets who were before you.

What Do Trailblazers – Old Saints - Offer?

What advice can old witnesses give to a son or grandson like you? People whose hands are now wrinkled and folded!

First, allow the Holy Spirit to guide and teach you through your process. God is always in control. Remember that He knows everything, even when you cannot understand or see the steps in your journey. Lean on Him for strength and direction in the matter.

Second, it is ok to acknowledge your emotions. Part of the process involves recognizing your feelings. Your feelings are real. God knows every range of your emotions. You will not surprise Him.

God indeed allows things to happen. He is not to blame for evil. Nevertheless, nothing happens without His approval. God does not cause wrong. He is Sovereign; He is holy; He is righteousness. He is against evil, and He can turn what was meant for evil to bless you in these times so that the Word of God strengthens your resolve and others. He can make your circumstances benefit not only you but also others. God can do this.

Listen to what He has to say about your circumstance, i.e., in Psalm 91:1; 9-12 NIV, *Whoever dwells in the shelter of the Most High…If you say, "The Lord is my refuge," and you make the Most High your dwelling, no harm will overtake you, and no disaster will come near your tent. For he will command his angels concerning you to guard you in all your ways; they will lift you in their hands so that you will not strike your foot against a stone.*

Is your peace dependent on someone else's? No. It is how you handle the crisis in Him (God).

God always operates to support and improve the well-being of His people. Why? He is Holy and cannot lie. Your circumstances will become a testimony that strengthens God's glory.

Third, examine your motives. What is the overwhelming motivating factor for your action(s)? What is your prevailing desire? Is it to please God *or* man? Proverbs 16:1-2 NIV says, *'To humans belong the plans of the heart, but from the Lord comes the proper answer of the tongue. All a person's ways seem pure to them, but the Lord weighs motives. In their hearts, humans plan their course, but the Lord establishes their steps (verse 9)."*

Are your plans persuaded by the deceitfulness of man? Do you answer to man's ways? Whom will your actions honor? Are you listening to God concerning your peace in matters of the heart? Do you bring glory to God and have wisdom from Him?

In another version of that chapter, Proverbs 16:22-24 ESV says, *"Good sense is a fountain of life to him who has it, but the instruction of fools is folly. The heart of the wise makes his speech judicious (that is, with good judgment) and adds persuasiveness to his lips. Gracious words are like a honeycomb, sweetness to the soul and health to the body."*

It is scientifically proven that an unhealthy spirit will breed unhealthy conditions. An unhealthy spirit causes people to suffer physically, emotionally, financially, psychologically, and spiritually.

Fourth, consider the order of your affairs. The scripture of Matthew 3:33 NIV reads, "But seek first his kingdom and his righteousness, and all these things will be given to you as well." Is that possible? Is it possible that in your affairs, your thoughts should come from God so that He is allowed to bring you into a plan of order and not chaos? The saints of God would readily answer, "Yes." They have been recipients of miracles and know that His resources will be available for all resources belong to Him. That is why they stand on verse 34 in this passage, *"Therefore do not worry about tomorrow, for tomorrow will worry about itself. Each day has enough trouble of its own."* In due season, you will reap the good fruit of your labor. There is work to be done in a season, my son.

An analogy is that of a farmer. The farmer prepares the soil for planting the seeds. He tends to the seed by providing the nourishment it needs to grow. He will reap the harvest in due season. Harvest time and planting times differ; God will give the increase. Believe in the Word when it says, "It is better to be of a lowly spirit with the poor than to divide the spoil with the proud" Proverbs 16:19 NKJV. Seek God first, my child, for an abundant life, and allow Him to generate blessings for your inheritance.

Finally, avoid the foolish talk of the unwise. It is ridiculous to argue with unwise men. Do not try to reason with fools; they are unreasonable. Their motives are impure. They operate at the "ground level" without understanding your higher call. Observe and listen for Truth.

My son, the spirit of the eagle, is in you; it is the spirit of a warrior, or a survivor, who can discern from a distance.

You cannot make a crow (a foolish person) an eagle. In dealing with a crow or *buzzard mentality*, you must rise above such behaviors for your peace.

The scripture in Isaiah 40:30-31 NKJV tells us that: *Even youths shall faint and be weary, and young men shall fall exhausted, but they who wait for the Lord shall renew their strength; they shall mount up with wings like eagles; they shall run and not be weary; they shall walk and not faint.*

Yes, appreciate the operation of good sense. Some things are not spiritual. God is interested in changing you more than changing your circumstances. You function in a natural world; you are in the world, as Jesus was. Jesus recognized what was natural from that which was spiritual. For example, you pay for bread with money. Operate in understanding and respecting the differences. Discerning what is natural and spiritual requires a connection with the Holy Spirit.

Life's Nugget - Remember, the challenge of peace is how you handle the crisis -the storm- when it looks more prominent than you.

For Sons and Grandsons - The Legacy You Deserve

Personal picture captured of one of my grandsons with a life-like figure of one of his still favorite players, Kobe Bryant. Challenges in life are real. Being in the game makes you successful - Go "JoJo!"

Chapter 4

It is possible to cherish both.

MARRIAGE VERSUS PARENTHOOD

It is the laughter that subdues the tears.

God, in his infinite wisdom, created us with an array of emotions. He knew this array was needed for different circumstances in these relationships.

I think that outside of marriage, no other relationship will challenge you as much as parenthood. In both, you have the opportunity to exercise all of your emotions. Yes, you will use the stretch of your imagination. Know, however, you must ask God for wisdom and protection of these institutions.

God established marriage and parenthood as part of the family. God loves the family. Within the family are individuals, uniquely designed persons. We often say so, but living as a unit of individuals can be frustrating and rewarding.

It can be frustrating when individuals find it difficult to express their feelings, especially if they have no voice. It will require considerable effort to work together as a unit. God expects men to cooperate with the Holy Spirit to lead the unit. So, I urge you to choose wisely regarding marriage and parenthood. God uses the family as a unit for multiplying (replenishing) the earth. God's standard for marriage and parenting remains unchanged. The chain of command, with God as the top CEO, is the foundation of an excellent relationship for demonstrating love (Genesis 1; Ephesians 4).

Seek Him for the love, care, support, honor, trust, wisdom, and understanding of your needs. After all, God created, can subdue, and maintain His creation.

Taken from the NIV (New International Version) Bible, these scriptures read as follows:

I John 4:19

We love because he first loved us.

I Corinthians 13:4-7

Love is patient; love is kind. It does not envy; it does not boast, it is not proud.
It does not dishonor others, is not self-seeking, is not easily angered, and keeps no record of wrongs.
Love does not delight in evil but rejoices with the truth.
It always protects, always trusts, always hopes, and always perseveres.

Acts 2:10

He and all his family were devout and God-fearing, giving generously to those in need and praying to God regularly.

Psalm 127:3-5

Children are a heritage from the LORD, offspring a reward from him.
Like arrows in the hands of a warrior are children born in one's youth.

Blessed is the man whose quiver is full of them. They will not be put to shame when they contend with their opponents in court.

Colossians 3:20

Children, obey your parents in everything, for this pleases the Lord.

Ephesians 6:1-2

Children, obey your parents in the Lord, for this is right.

Honor your father and mother"—which is the first commandment with a promise—

I Timothy 3:4

He must manage his own family well and see that his children obey him, and he must do so in a manner worthy of full respect.

I Timothy 5:8

Anyone who does not provide for their relatives, especially their own household, has denied the faith and is worse than an unbeliever.

Colossians 3:19

Husbands, love your wives and do not be harsh with them.

In short, *I extend these "Nuggets of Growth" for wellness in Him, even to other generations.*

Your Proverbial Mom

*A parent's legacy can live on - Blessings of a third-generation
God allows for different events in our seasons!*

Chapter 5

Solitude (a Royal_night_life Photography)

UNDERSTANDING YOUR SPIRIT-MAN

The Father in heaven created you with a soul, body, and spirit. There are many verses in the Bible about the purpose or function of each. I write this message to you, my son, because, as I recall, even as a youngster and into my adult years, I am still learning things about the body, soul, and spirit. Over time, these terms have continued to change and evolve, which may be a good reason why many teachers avoid them.

Genesis 2:7 NIV states, " then the LORD God formed the man of dust from the ground and breathed into his nostrils the breath of life, and the man became a living creature. Oftentimes, as a young disciple of God, I found it difficult to understand some of the directives given from the pulpit; yet I trusted in what was being hurled from the man of God as he spoke. You grow as a Christian through learning Truth.

One scripture that the pastor often cited at the end of the church service was from 1 Thessalonians 5:23 NIV: *May God Himself, the God of peace, sanctify you through and through. May your whole spirit, soul, and body be kept blameless at the coming of our Lord Jesus Christ.* What was he talking about? I listened to the Sunday School teachers because I wanted to know more about the "three parts" of me, which they said God created us with: a physical body, a mind for gaining knowledge, and a spirit patterned after the Maker. Yet, as much as I desired to know from them, more questions remained and were problematic in some ways because there was not much teaching about the spirit of man. I hope to provide you with at least a starting point from which to build in these few pages.

Understanding the body and soul will aid in understanding and appreciating the spiritual progression of the human being. Physically, we can observe that the body grows and matures as it ages. As babies, we drink liquid food before eating solids or meat. Educationally, we progress from grade to grade; we do not start in twelfth grade; instead, we move from pre-kindergarten and upward, adding to our knowledge and advancement. We can observe this progression in nature.

How does the soul differ from the spirit of man? Our soul contains the emotions we feel. Just as God feels emotions, so do we. Unlike God, our soul needs to rest. Jesus invited us to the type of rest that we need for our souls. Matthew 11:28-29 NIV, *Come to me, all you who are weary and burdened, and I will give you rest. Take my yoke upon you and learn from me, for I am gentle and humble in heart, and you will find rest for your souls.*

We become emotionally and physically exhausted from life's struggles; one can easily feel overwhelmed and burdened. In nature, a yoke, for example, is a type of harness that is placed around the neck of two animals so they can walk/pull together as one in unity. Jesus invites the weary soul to come to Him so that He can carry that burden. The two become one unit in carrying the load. He lifts the believer from feeling overburdened. His load is light and easy...*For my burden is light and easy (v 30).*

Accepting Jesus to take this yoke means you move forward with power because the soul is at rest in Him. You become comforted concerning your circumstances because you have confidence in Him, of Him, by Him, and for Him.

Before you understood what it meant to walk in Christ, you were guided by rules from adults, i.e., your parents, teachers, and community standards. You were aware of right and wrong due to these rules and your consciousness/subconsciousness capacity – that inner voice. As you matured, you fed your faith in God. You developed a personal relationship with Christ. This new life is because of what Christ did for you. It is in this new life that the Holy Spirit has come into your heart to guide, teach, and rule your spirit man. You are more concerned about pleasing God than yourself. Your tactics of operation have changed. The spirit-man seeks righteousness as God desires and not what the *self desires*. The Bible says the Spirit knows the things of God; therefore, to be comforted by the Spirit will bring your spirit the power to rest the soul, to be anxious for nothing because God cares for you (trust).

Affirming Who You Are – Affirmations

David, the shepherd boy, learned as a warrior, as a servant of God, and as the King of the nation of Israel to affirm his position in life. He wrote affirmations such as *"The Lord is my shepherd, and I shall not want; the Lord is my light and my refuge, whom shall I fear? The Lord is my high tower.* So should you, my son. Affirm each day that God gives you with affirmations of faith that you are under the protection of the Almighty. Feel just as intensely in feeding your spiritual man as you do in feeding your physical body. One day, your spirit man will leave your physical body.

The Spirit-Man Takes Flight

Ecclesiastes 12:7 NIV states, ' and the dust returns to the earth as it was, and the spirit returns to God who gave it.' Read and study the Word of God for your spiritual nourishment, looking forward to that flight.

Finally, in Hebrews 4:12 NIV, "For the word of God is alive and active. Sharper than any double-edged sword, it penetrates even to dividing soul and spirit, joints and marrow; it judges the thoughts and attitudes of the heart." Daily, let your heart's desire be known. Ask the Holy Spirit for teaching and guidance as you travel toward that flight.

Chapter 6

Majestic. (a Royal_night_life Photography)

THE GIFT IS MORE THAN THE PAIN.

When I think about the birth of my children and their children, I know that the gift is more than the labor pains.

I would not change anything about the pain of labor if it meant I could not have these precious jewels in our lives.

Travailing that fostered triumphantly

Many mothers would agree that the physical pain of childbirth leads to a miraculous, unexplainable sense of joy in the face of their newborn. In Genesis 3:16, God told Eve that childbirth would be physically painful. He explained that her sorrow and conception would be multiplied. Even in their old age, God prospered Adam and Eve so that they could bear more children (Genesis 5). The Bible says that God blessed them as Mankind on the day they were created. So, how can the gift be more than the pain?

Heartbreaking Pain

Pain and blessings are a part of this earthly life.

Elizabeth, the mother of John the Baptist, and Mary, the mother of Jesus, felt this pain that leaves you feeling helpless. Can you imagine the pain these mothers felt in knowing that their children would suffer unjustly because of the unrighteousness of men? Knowing that their children's death was part of God's plan, it had to be both joyous and devastating. Still, the joy of pregnancy and the gift of life did not make Elizabeth, Zacharias, Mary, or Joseph regret their roles in carrying out God's plan of salvation. The gift of life was more than the pain.

Perhaps every family can tell of that one particular heartbreaking pain when one feels so devastated about the passing of a loved one – i.e., the loss of a child, mother, father, close relative, or friend. It is an interruption in your life cycle like no other. It is not for a few days that you feel this pain – it seems like a lifetime. Nevertheless, the scriptures tell us that there is no suffering that Jesus does not understand. Yes, even Jesus experienced this type of pain and shed tears.

Jesus, when he heard about his cousin John's death, felt the pain of loss for this beloved family member (Matthew 14); yet it did not keep Jesus from carrying out the will of his heavenly Father. Then there was a time when Jesus cried in agony at the thought of being separated from his heavenly Father. He knew that, in suffering the special death for sin, he would suffer the pain of separation from his heavenly Father while on the cross. He prayed in the Garden of Gethsemane for this bitter cup (this assignment) to pass him by (Matthew 26:39). Yet, God's love for Mankind would not change the fate or cause of Jesus's suffering on the cross to bring humanity back into fellowship with God. The gift to us is greater than any of the pain.

Over the years, I have listened to countless sons and grandsons in my roles as an educator, minister, mother, grandmother, mentor, and friend. Many sons and grandsons are troubled by their "broken" relationships with their mothers and fathers. Some of them had no relationship with their biological fathers; some blamed their mothers for their feelings of abandonment. Then some spoke of their desire to be better fathers, despite their parents' shortcomings, family dysfunctions, and dynamics.

It is safe to say that our God views humanity as His creation and is dedicated to protecting and loving us. The dynamics and care are natural and play out in everyday life. Each day, God gives us new mercy. What a gift! This is a further demonstration of his love despite our actions and inactions. His new mercy (to all) is an example of the grace of God. It is an unmerited favor. This means we do not deserve this favor from Him, but He does this for His children.

How can you show such love toward others so that His gift is more than pain? The goal is to please the Heavenly Father.

Some people find it difficult to move forward because of their suffering. Some are fueled by anger. Some find refuge in placing blame on others for their state in life. Some choose to "drop out" of life. Some turn to substance abuse and abusive relationships. However, God has declared that Mankind was worth saving.

Satan does not want people to be saved. He has led too many to believe in hopelessness. He continues to function in the minds of people with this same lie. On the other hand, God has a gift that is more than any pain. He offers Jesus Christ to anyone. Believing in the Christ who can save your soul, who will aid you in this cycle of life, is a gift of salvation from God. It means asking God to forgive you of all your sins. You are sorry for sinning against Him. You want Jesus Christ, His son, to come into your life and govern your life by the Holy Spirit, in the name of Jesus. Immediately, you receive the gift.

The enemy does not want people to believe that acquiring this Gift from God is that simple. He wants people to focus more on the pain and suffering than on the One who can provide the necessary support for survival in life.

God operates in our blessings amid storms. He provides water in desert places, calms the deepest storms, and supplies cattle on the mountaintop.

Sum Total

It is totally up to you to accept God's gift to the world, which will help you bear your pain.

Jesus said, "Very truly I tell you, no one can see the kingdom of God unless they are born again" (John 3:3, NIV). Also, in John 3:16-21, "For God so loved the world that he gave his only Son, that whoever believes in him should not perish but have eternal life. God did not send his Son into the world to condemn the world, but for the world to be saved through him. Whoever believes in him is not condemned, but whoever does not believe is condemned already because he has not believed in the name of the only Son of God. And this is the judgment: the light has come into the world, and people loved the darkness rather than the light because their works were evil. Everyone who does wicked things hates the light and does not come to light, lest his works should be exposed. But whoever does what is true comes to light so that it may be seen that his works have been carried out in God."

Your decision.

Chapter 7

You can stand tall and strong like this tree. The photo was taken on one of my morning prayer walks. A tribute to every son and grandson.

MY DEAR

My Dear,

I thought you needed to know what I love about you. Yes, Nana indeed loves you because you are part of my legacy, but there are also reasons beyond that that make it easier to love you. I love you for the person you are.

I watch you grow from a baby into the young man you are. I am proud to say to anyone that you are my grandson.

You are genuine. You are honest about your limitations and challenges, and you fight to overcome them. You are touched by the things you see happening around you because you care about others. Your caring has made a difference in some of our most complex challenges as a family.

You are a humble person; you are NOT arrogant. God requires that of us – to show humanity towards one another. God calls it humility. You set an example as one who learns from mistakes and grows.

I listen when you speak of your goals –the importance of a vision. You are realistic. "Yes, for I **know the plans** I have for you," says the LORD. "They are **plans** for good, not disaster, to give you a future and hope."

I admire your courage. You possess the fortitude of a soldier and the wisdom of a wise leader. You take risks for the good of a situation.

I admire how you do not hold grudges; you have consoled others who have made mistakes and encouraged them not to give up.

You are not afraid of your share of responsibilities; instead, you view it as a part of moving toward your vision.

I have watched you graciously accept rewards for your academic and athletic achievements and be just as excited about the success of others.

I pray that God will continue to help you utilize your gifts and talents and provide you with clear direction in your decision-making for the good of serving the kingdom. I pray that God's grace and mercy continue to be granted to you; I pray that you use the power and authority of God in your position(s) to always be a blessing for your own development and the benefit of others.

May you always cooperate with the Holy Spirit to lead you; this will please the Father.

And finally, my dear grandson, I pray you will continue to act with wisdom and obedience to God as a servant leader, giving God all the glory.

With my love,

Your Proverbial Nana

Encouragement

Dear Son,

You can meet life's challenges as long as you walk with God. He is our hope and strength. Remember, in all these things we are more than conquerors (Romans 8:37 NIV). God's word will not fail.

Pray daily. Read the word, for it is power and inspiration. Faith in God is our higher power. Call on him every day. He loved you before you were placed in the belly of your mother. With compassion and mercy, he will raise you.

In your prayers, give him praise and thanksgiving. The earth is the Lord's and everything in it (Psalm 24:1). He formed the heavens and earth. He founded the seas and established the waters also. God is a good Father. Everything that has breath, must praise the Lord. Even Jesus Christ is at the right hand of the Father interceding for us. The Lord is the strength of his children. Sing the praises of the Lord. He does not require elaborate words. You worship by living for him. When you enter the house of prayer, worship him with a sincere heart. This pleases the Lord.

Praise be to God, for he has and will hear your cry.

Chapter 8

Success calls for PREPARATION before the game starts!

HOW DO YOU BREAK THROUGH?

My son, thank you for teaching me about the strategizing of the game of football. As I listened to you, I saw the excitement and passion you have for the game. What's more, I equate natural sports with spiritual practices in how you must approach life.

God's strategy differs from that of the enemy, the opposer. Satan's strategies are directed toward confusion, false accusations, robbery, and destruction of the believer who places their faith in God. On the other hand, God's strategy will bring victory for the believer, bringing glory to God. I pray that, among our many conversations, this is one that you will remember. God's plan, in the natural realm, may seem illogical, but it works.

I can recall many examples from the Bible and from personal experiences as evidence. Just as you strategize for the best offensive and defensive plays for each game (battle), you must do so in life.

You have taught me that in strategizing for a game, one must take stock of how one prepares for each battle in pursuit of victory.

First, one must be conscious of how one suits up. I paid special attention to the word "suit-up." The details were in the message of preparation – the equipment. The helmet, shoulder pad, and mouthpiece provide protection. The mouthpiece has a guard attached to it. There is an uncovered area that allows you to see where you are going and what is coming toward you. The jersey and pants identify the players. There are numbers (1-99) on the back of each player's jersey, and these numbers are often designated to be used for specific position assignments. For example, numbers:

#1-9 Quarter Backs/Punters/Kickers

#10-19 Quarter Backs/Punters/Kickers/Wide Receivers

#20-29 Corner Backs/Running Backs/Safeties

#30-39 Corner Backs/Running Backs/Safeties

#40-49 Corner Backs/Running Backs/Safeties/Tight Ends

#50-59 Defensive Linemen/Offensive Linemen/Line Backer

#60-69 Defensive Linemen/Offensive Linemen

#70-79 Defensive Linemen/Offensive Linemen

#80-89 Tight End/Wide Receiver

#90-99 Defensive Linemen/Line Backer

Moreover, I recall you mentioning that in college and professional football, rules are associated with specific numbers.

You also told me that special material is recommended for the pants. Patches are sewn into specific uniforms as a means of communication to the players; audio pieces can be attached to the helmet, making it easier to hear the coach when the crowd is screaming. There are even special temperature suits to help regulate the heat. Consideration is also given to the footwear, i.e., playing on turf or grass, as well as weather conditions (rain, sunshine, snow). Footwear changes may even occur while playing the game. If conditions change, the players' footwear may change. Make the required adjustments.

The team's manager works to select and organize the players for each game. The manager, like the players, must be aware of the strengths of his team and the opponents. For instance, there must be awareness of the challenges that the opposition may impose on your team's defeat. The manager must consider the team's willingness to play and their effective teamwork to achieve victory.

Yes, the game has a spiritual connection. You see, in life, you must be suited, too. Ephesians 6:10-13 provides a description of the attire for the believer. The believer is pictured as a soldier. The soldier wears cleats designed to provide firm footing against the enemy and to facilitate movement on rugged terrain. The shield of faith strengthens the inner spirit of a man; it is provided through the Holy Spirit. The Holy Spirit is there to help the soldier in producing good fruit that is the result of a change in the heart. In the heart is the root of love (Ephesians 3:16-19). This love is beyond knowledge. The love works a power in the soldier that glorifies the Father. God calls the plays. As part of His team, the soldier can rest in Christ. The one who gets the glory is not the soldier; all the glory belongs to the Father (the Chief Commander).

As to the soldier's equipment, there are attachments to the helmet as well. The attachment for the believing soldier is to hold things in place, with the helmet providing protection. In the spiritual realm, God, the Father, protects the soldier from the enemy. That is why you, as a soldier, can continue to stand and break through challenges. The Lord is your protector. In Ephesians 6:14-20, the soldier realizes that God has given him the strength to stand up and persevere, allowing the believing soldier to speak boldly as is appropriate. This is the wisdom that God gives to those who ask of Him. This type of wisdom frees you, as a soldier, from chains of defeat because your reliance is totally on Him and not on your physical strength.

From the Scriptures, I would like to recount some of the extraordinary stories of victories that God has given to mere men who listened and obeyed the strategies of God. God gave them miraculous strategies. Miraculous strategies are the ones that cannot be accomplished by reason of man. For instance, Joshua 6:6-27 is the story of how the children of Israel won the battle against their enemy. On the seventh time that the children walked around the enemy's city, they were to bellow a loud shout when they heard the sound of the soldiers' trumpets. As instructed, they were obedient to God, and the wall of the enemy miraculously came down, allowing them to take the city by victory.

In Judges 7, Gideon, a valiant soldier, listened to God and fought against the enemy with only 300 warriors. What a triumph that was.

In 2 Kings 5:10, Elisha, a prophet of God, instructs a man of leprosy (skin disease) to dip himself in the Jordan River seven times. In nature, it did not make sense, but God healed the man because of the man's faith and obedience to follow those instructions. In 2 Chronicles 20, the victorious story of Jehoshaphat and the people of Judah and Jerusalem is recorded.

Over and over, God demonstrates how to break through for victory. Being obedient to God brings miraculous strategies for breakthrough. Following God's plan is different from that of mere men, and His strategy for victory is meant for believers who have faith in Him.

There is a pronounced strategy of God. So, how will you break through? You will suit up with faith in God and obedience to Him. God says that the Holy Spirit will teach you – greater is He that is in you than he (that old devil) in the world. So, my son, for every battle…

May the God of peace, who through the blood of the eternal covenant brought back from the dead our Lord Jesus, that great Shepherd of the sheep, equip you, my son, with everything good for doing his will, and may he work in you what is pleasing to him, through Jesus Christ to whom be glory forever and ever.

Chapter 9

Life is a presentation style with meaning. It has purpose. It speaks through our images and presentations. (a Royal_night_life Photograph)

WHEN YOU LOOK LIKE YOUR DADDY

I get that you are mad. Someone stopped you in your tracks and said, "You look like your daddy.".

Maybe you wanted to punch the person out, or perhaps you were glad to say, "Thank you." Not everyone appreciates this statement as a compliment.

Some young boys are doing all they can to avoid being like their Daddy. Then, some strive to mirror their fathers. Whatever the case, it is a testament to one way or another. When I heard my brother's sermon, I was flooded with memories of our Dad.

Even for me, not all the memories of Dad make me happy. However, I am grateful for the thoughts he provided and insisted that we follow, even if he was disobedient at times too (we all are). As we grew up, we were more aware that God was our dad's guiding light. We have the promise of God that we will see Dad again because those who die in Christ only transition from the earth to eternal life.

Think about this. Why would a person be upset or thankful if they are told that they look like your daddy? It seems that much of the daily conversation between young boys and older men is colorful and generational.

Data generated from research centers, such as Pew Research, show that many males are deprived of positive friendships and guidance by their biological fathers. Too many males feel lost because they do not know their fathers as guiding lights in their lives. Some experience loss from "poisonous" relationships that create cycles of abuse. Some of this pain comes from the bitterness of biological mothers who pass along their hurt because of the negative relationships or lack thereof with their fathers or the son's father. What are sons to do?

First, it is OK to acknowledge that your emotional pain is real. Why? Hurting people hurt other people. Physical scars are easily noticeable, but emotional scars can be hidden so deeply that they can manifest in deadly ways. More than you (we) know, these hurting people become *professionals* in disguising their emotional pain. From the outside, they look as though they have it "going on." Internally, they are hurting - damaged.

Acknowledging the pain can start the healing process. Quiet people are most noticeable when it comes to depression; it is the talkative ones who can easily go unnoticed. In both situations, recognizing that you are hurting cannot only help you but also help others. It is a wise decision to seek professional help so that you can effectively address your feelings. God has servant leaders in the business of professional Christian counseling.

Note that sometimes the person may not be aware of the root cause of their pain. Neglecting your emotional health is personal abuse. It can lead to negative thoughts that are passed on for generations. You may have heard others refer to the negative actions of others, i.e., dysfunction in families. So, do not be surprised if you encounter people who resent your saying, "You look like your dad."

Second, realize that the root cause of your pain might be a failure to forgive yourself and others. Physicians have found that stress is a leading cause of heart disease and is problematic to other diseases, i.e., cancer. And many of these diseases are the effects of childhood trauma – the type of trauma that is compounded over time, that was not addressed. According to these researchers, mental health is one of the leading causes of crime, leading to massive incarceration in the United States (Pew Research Center on Crime).

Statistically, in our society, more males lead the majority of ministries (Pastoralcounseling.org). They are in leadership positions where congregations expect more and more from pastors and leaders. Thus, many pastors chose to leave ministries because of the demands. Still, others give more attention to ministry as a means of escaping personal issues, staying too busy. Their emotional wounds are left unhealed, bound up without the necessary healing.

Society has even encouraged males to get over personal issues and look strong, so they put up walls of defense to shield themselves from family, friends, and other communities of support. This phenomenon occurs in many institutions and industries, such as the entertainment industry. Burying yourself at any type of work (and school is work) is not the answer to healing from emotional pain, either.

Beyond recognizing that your hurt is real and identifying the root cause of your pain, what more can you do?

God as My Father

Your peace will not come through others nor from riches. Riches do not fill a diseased heart. The gap, the void, will still exist unless you connect to the Source – your Father – Your Abba – Your Daddy. All of the above require you to seek the Source for healing.

God's Holy Spirit is available to work with you through this process. To look like your real Daddy, your spiritual Father is better than any biological father.

I heard my brother declare on that particular Sunday in June, "*I do not mind when someone tells me that you look like your Daddy.* In fact, I say, "Thank you," because I desire to emulate my Spiritual Father. I appreciate those who tell me that my dad was proud of me; I do. But in the end, I want to hear my spiritual Father say, "Well done, thy good and faithful servant. Come in. You have been faithful to a few things, and now I will make you a ruler over greater things." That is the Father I want to look most like, even on earth. I want to look like the Father who loves me more than anyone else. The Father who provides for me amazingly. The Father who gave His only begotten

Son so that I can live an abundant life. This is the Father I can go to at midnight, who hears my crying heart, gives me comfort, and tells me that He is always available. This is the One who challenges me to be better to others for His sake while providing for me. I want to look like my Daddy, my Heavenly Father."

I'd like to share with you a story I heard decades ago. It is the story of an old man and a young boy.

The Old Man and Young Boy

A little boy was asked to learn the 23rd Psalm for an upcoming church program. He was thrilled to be asked. He worked very hard to learn the scripture. Finally, the day came for him to recite the scripture:

The Lord is my shepherd; I shall not want.
He makes me lie down in green pastures;
He leads me beside the still waters.
He restores my soul; He leads me in the paths of righteousness
For His name's sake.
Yea, though I walk through the valley of the shadow of death,
I will fear no evil, For You are with me.
Your rod and Your staff, they comfort me.
You prepare a table before me in the presence of my enemies;
You anoint my head with oil; My cup runs over.
Surely goodness and mercy shall follow me, all the days of my life, and I will dwell in the house of the Lord - Forever.

At the end of the little boy's recitation (reciting of the scripture), the church clapped for him. They were so proud that this little child was brave enough to stand before the audience and recite the scripture loudly. He did a great job.

As the little boy took his seat, an old man in the corner of the church stood up. It was obvious that the old man was having difficulty standing. So, one of the men near him gently took hold of the old man's arm. With a walking cane and the support of another's help, the old man moved forward. Then the old man lifted up his head and began to say the words of the 23rd Psalm. As he spoke, tears streamed down the old man's face. At some point in speaking, he lifted up his arm and waved his hands. He continued, but slowly, until he had finished the words of the scripture.

The little boy noticed that many of the people in the church were silently crying. Such seemed to be chatting under their breath. The little boy noticed that even his mother was sobbing too. It took a while, but eventually, the preacher stood before the church, once the old man sat down. It was obvious to the little boy that the minister was crying as well.

After church, the little boy asked the program planner, "Why did the old man cry when he recited the 23rd Psalm? And why did the people clap for me but cry when the old man recited the scripture?"

The program planner replied, "You see, son, you did a great job. You recited the scripture so bravely and made us very proud of you. The difference is, you know the words of the scripture, but the old man knows the Shepherd."

"It is my prayer, too, that you want to look like that spiritual daddy – the Great Shepherd. Believing and seeking Him for all your healing, including your spiritual and emotional healing. When you look like my Daddy..."

Chapter 10

"The strength that I can do this comes from within! Procrastination does not bring victory. It slows the process." – The Author [Self]

BUILDING

If I ask you to draw a picture representing your life, what would it include? If I ask you to draw a picture of what you are willing to share with others, what would it be? Is it a picture of what you treasure? Is it replaceable? Is it constructive? Is it worth more than money? Would you want to live without it? Is it part of your legacy that is worthy of leaving behind for someone to treasure? Is it a showpiece, or will it bring peace? Is it representative of who you are or desire to be?

A Perspective on Building

When a carpenter decides to build, he examines the tools needed for the job. He estimates the cost. He considers the timeframe for completing the job. He gathers the materials to begin the project and keeps track of what he needs to manage it until completion.

Each of us has the task of building. Jesus's earthly father, Joseph, was a carpenter. I imagine that as a child, Jesus and his siblings were taught the value of family tools and the care one must take in handling them.

As children, our dad taught us about the value of his tools and the care we must take when handling them. We were not allowed to use any tool without first getting his permission. However, over time, each of us was given a small toolset after proving to be worthy (responsible) stewards. Even today, I have my own toolset. In a small but significant way, Dad passed on part of this legacy to us. We created with our hands, inspired as *little carpenter*s. We grew up wanting to improve or fix things after watching and learning from him.

Spiritually Speaking

Do you view God as a builder? Do you believe that He is the Creator of all things? Do you think God is the reason or the blame for the chaos in this world? Do you believe that, as the Creator, God is standing on the sidelines watching the "show?" Do you value God? Do you value the legacy He passed on – fellowship? What part, if any, do you believe that God plays in the affairs of this world?

These are a few fair questions that come to mind when people talk about our Sovereign God as the One who is in Control yet gives us free will to choose. No one has all the answers when it comes to our Sovereign God. With all the different gods being discussed, debated, and presented in our society today, it takes faith to believe in the Almighty Creator of the heavens and earth on this journey. The Holy Scriptures are a part of our legacy and an essential part of our evidence for building faith in Him. The Holy Spirit is part of our legacy to build us up. *"When the Spirit of truth comes, he will guide you into all the truth, for he will not speak on his own authority, but whatever he hears he will speak, and he will declare to you the things that are to come. That is why we stand on the Word*, John 16:13 ESV.

Building a Strong Foundation.

Genesis 1, the first book of the Bible, describes God's actions in this regard. Verses 26-28 NKJV state, *"Then God said, 'Let Us make man in Our image, according to Our likeness; let them have dominion over the fish of the sea, over the birds of the air, and over the cattle, over all the earth and over every creeping thing that creeps on the earth." So God created man in His own image; in the image of God He created him; male and female He created them. Then God blessed them, and God said to them, "Be fruitful and multiply; fill the earth and subdue it; have dominion over the fish of the sea, over the birds of the air, and over every living thing that moves on the earth."* This means that we are accountable (responsible) for tending this garden.

Believing that God is the Creator of all things puts you in the position of a builder. How so? He gave man dominion over the earth.

Jesus taught about building. Matthew 7:24-27 ESV, "Everyone then who hears these words of mine and does them will be like a wise man who built his house on the rock. And the rain fell, and the floods came, and the winds blew and beat on that house, but it did not fall, because it had been founded on the rock. And everyone who hears these words of mine and does not do them will be like a foolish man who built his house on the sand. And the rain fell, and the floods came, and the winds blew and beat against that house, and it fell, and great was the fall of it."

That is why building a legacy is so important. Every day, you paint a picture to leave. It is a picture of the house that you are building.

Are you building up what represents who you aspire to be? Will the treasures in your house be worth leaving for generations to come? You are the builder.

When the wind blows, will your house stand up? The songwriter said, "My hope is built on a solid foundation. That foundation is Jesus Christ." If you build on this rock, the promise from the Creator is that you will have a solid foundation for building upward and outward. He has promised to be the rock of the ages. The ancient songwriter wrote, "I have been young, and now am old, yet I have not seen the righteous forsaken or his children begging for bread," Psalm 37:25 ESV.

Allowing Him to be the architect of your life means the picture that you draw should look brighter and stronger. The construction of the building is robust, ensuring it will stand strong for generations to come. Build up and out for His glory!

Chapter 11

"Wisdom starts developing in the early years for a lifetime of lessons." – The Author [Self]

WISDOM IS MORE THAN KNOWLEDGE

Feed yourself from the wisdom bank -

I remember, as a child, watching my father work on different types of automobiles – his car, neighbors', and others. He was not a mechanic by trade, but a gifted one. People would even drive from other areas after hearing about his expertise. He could fix things. He did not have car manuals to guide him, but he relied on his skill set, which was driven by a systematic process, until he resolved the issue. That was wisdom.

His father, my grandfather, was one who, by nature, accepted challenges such as these equally. He could not read but was great at remembering details. I was an adult when I found out that he was illiterate. He was very good at masking it. He even owned a community store in the neighborhood. He could perform simple math calculations and write his name. He drove a car and held a valid driver's license. He spoke extensively about the Bible. He loved listening to the children read aloud to him. I am even more amazed when I think about how he utilized practical skills to navigate the literary society around him, as his survival depended on his talents and wisdom. Moreover, he was not the only man in the neighborhood who did not read.

For years, we, as neighborhood children, were not aware that the church pastor could not read. He could write his name, and people respected his counsel.

I recall how the pastor's wife would read the scripture aloud as he repeated. This was known as lining the scriptures. The pastor was even able to call her attention to a mistake by simply saying, "Look at that again." She would smile and reread it.

The Sunday school superintendent was a highly respected man in the community – a person who taught the neighborhood children about right and wrong, who was held up as an example of a good family man, a hard worker, and a man who loved the Lord. He always spoke in a kind yet stern voice when disciplining children, never shouting. When he died, there were tears from the men in the community as much as there were from the children and mothers. Thus, the question becomes, "What made others see these men as men of great talent and wisdom?"

The definition of wisdom is often equated with intelligence in our society and is usually associated with an extraordinary display of work, such as Picasso's paintings. The men mentioned above did not paint like the famous Picasso, nor did they build a wall like the Great Wall of China. They are not found in history books, yet they were considered men of wisdom among many they served. So why were they viewed as men of wisdom? These men received such recognition because they were present in the lives of those they were honored to serve. The people received them as teachers, mentors, counselors, craftsmen, and providers. They were present not only to serve but also to share the wisdom that God imparted to them for the betterment of the community and for their family members. They listened and learned from one another to build stronger offshoots among families. They encouraged the love of God. Because of these connections, we, as young children, learned valuable life lessons. They encouraged us to listen in school and obey our teachers, and learn something new every day. Their knowledge and wisdom were not from the books that they could not read with any amount of success, but it was from the wisdom bank of God.

Where Does Wisdom Come From and How Can You Receive It?

Knowledge is not wisdom. The questions concerning wisdom in Job 28:20-21 NIV read, *"Where then does wisdom come from? Where does understanding dwell?"* Verse 22 responds, "It is hidden from the eyes of every living thing, concealed even from the birds in the sky." God understands the way to it, and he alone knows where it dwells (verse 23). For he views the ends of the earth and sees everything under the heavens. When he established the force of the winds and measured out the waters, when he made a decree for the rain and a path for the thunderstorm, then he looked at wisdom and appraised it. He confirmed it and tested it, and he said to the human race, "The fear of the Lord – that is wisdom," Job 28:23-28 NIV. In wisdom, God has made all the earth, living things both small and great (Psalm 104:24 NIV).

Wisdom is priceless; it is worth more than rubies, gold, stocks, bonds, investments, etc.

Again, if any [man] lacks wisdom, you should ask God. *"But when you ask, you must believe and not doubt because the one who doubts is like a wave of the sea, blown and tossed by the winds. That person should not expect to receive anything from the Lord,"* James 1:6 NIV.

Consider this: if you ask for food from a parent, do you expect to receive it? Do you doubt that a loving parent would not give a hungry child the food he needs? The expectation is that the parent will feed the hungry child. God is wisdom.

God's Wisdom Brings Order

You, as God's child, my son, must ask God for His wisdom to guide you in every area of your life. In this world, mankind seeks to understand the world through various sciences. We categorize this order as studying humans, economics, governments, and ecological, biological, and technological systems. It is true that men have been abusive as caretakers in the world that God has given man dominion over. Still, as His people, we are obligated as citizens to be a blessing.

God gave you (us) the command to multiply on the earth as a blessing – operate as a servant leader. These systems are relevant in the territory where you will function and reside as His child. Yes, you can learn from a knowledge base of others, which is tied to your blessing, but it is God who gives the increase in you. How?

Man is endowed with creativity because man was created in the image of God. Man, however, has limitations because of his imagination. God placed these limitations as the Controller of the earth (Genesis 11). So, how is it that men continue to prosper in a world where he is limited by their own doing, where evil is present, where men seek to destroy their own kind, and where men continuously seek darkness rather than light? The answer is in God. Because of God's infinite wisdom, men of ordinary stature are blessed and will bless others for God's glory. God loves man. He created the things in this world for man's survival. Man does not create oxygen, dirt, trees, etc. These are examples of God's goodness and righteousness. Men who choose the wisdom of God do prosper. They have the promise of God that they rest in Him when they seek him; and even more, they enter into a place of rest eternally.

Rest and Unrest

The story of the rich man and Lazarus in Luke 16:19-24 NIV illustrates the contrast between the rest and unrest of two different men who died—one went to Hell, and the other was carried away by angels.

There was a rich man who was dressed in purple and fine linen and lived in luxury every day. At his gate was laid a beggar named Lazarus, covered with sores and longing to eat what fell from the rich man's table. Even the dogs came and licked his sores.

The time came when the beggar died, and the angels carried him to Abraham's side. The rich man also died and was buried. In Hades, where he was in torment, he looked up and saw Abraham far away, with Lazarus by his side. So he called him, 'Father Abraham, have pity on me and send Lazarus to dip the tip of his finger in water and cool my tongue because I am in agony in this fire.

But Abraham's response in verses 25-26 was,

> 'Son, remember that in your lifetime you received your good things, and likewise Lazarus evil things; but now he is comforted, and you are tormented. And besides all this, between us and you, there is a great gulf fixed so that those who want to pass from here to you cannot, nor can those from there pass to us."

God has prepared a place for those who are evil and a place for those who are righteous; this is in God's wisdom. It is God, alone, who created the wonders among, around, and for us. Just as He decided the beginning, He has the right to decide the ending of all. For those who choose not to shun His wisdom but rather seek His wisdom and understanding and live as His children, there is a crown of glory from Him that is everlasting.

Asking for Wisdom

If you ask my son to be endowed with the wisdom that represents God, you will be a wise and disciplined person on earth. James 1:5 NIV states, "If any of you lacks wisdom, you should ask God, who gives generously to all without finding fault, and it will be given to you." An example of this type of wisdom, characterized by order rather than chaos, is that of Solomon.

Solomon was a king in ancient Israel. He asked God for wisdom to govern the people of Israel with *justice, judgment, and equity.* The Bible describes Solomon's prayer for wisdom in 1 Kings 3:1-15. God honored Solomon's wish because of Solomon's unselfish request and the love that Solomon had in wanting to please the Lord.

There are many scriptures in the Bible that speak of God's wisdom being available to humanity. The Old Testament contains five books known as the Wisdom Books: *Job, Psalms, Ecclesiastes, Song of Solomon, and Proverbs.* In the New Testament, the apostles and disciples preached about God's wisdom. Recorded in Hebrews 1:1-4 NIV, "In the past, God spoke to our ancestors through the prophets at many times and in various ways, but in these last days he has spoken to us by his Son, whom he appointed heir of all things, and through whom also he made the universe. The Son is the radiance of God's glory and the exact representation of his being, sustaining all things by his powerful word. After he had provided purification for sins, he sat down at the right hand of Majesty in heaven. So he became as much superior to the angels as the name he has inherited is superior to theirs." This is the wisdom of God to save man through the Son and ask in the name of Jesus Christ.

Learning Wisdom

Finally, my son, learning wisdom is within your reach. A great deal of knowledge can be gained through proverbs, parables, and human experience. These provide the standard of living discussed in The Wisdom Books, which aims to teach moral character and how to live in society. God's wisdom is spiritual. In order to be preceptive servants, we must be able to discern Truth. This wisdom must be directed by the Holy Spirit. It is clear that Wisdom Books also provide instructions about listening; for listening is indeed important. Listening to hear from God means tuning your ears to what He is saying. Developing a listening ear aids in decision-making. That means praying for the ability to listen to the Holy Spirit is essential. If you want to live an abundant life, it means that you must prosper in the things of Christ for prosperous living. The biblical songwriter, Gimel, prayed in Psalm 119:18-19 NIV, *" Be good to your servant while I live that I may obey your word. Open my eyes [so]that I may see wonderful things in your law. I am a stranger on earth, do not hide your commands from me."* This songwriter understood his limitations, and he knew that instructions on how to live an abundant life must be directed by God, for prosperity is in God.

"Listen, my son, to your father's instruction, and do not forsake your mother's teaching," Proverbs 1:8 NIV. Why? False witnesses come in various forms at various times for various reasons. "The lips of the wise spread knowledge, but the hearts of fools are not upright," Proverbs 15:7.

"Good people obtain favor from the lord, but He condemns those who devise wicked schemes," Proverbs 12:2.

Those who are about God's agenda will be discerners of the Word so as not to cause harm and ruin, but they will bring order to your environment, i.e., family, workplace, community, and ministry. "An honest witness tells Truth, but a false witness tells lies, Proverbs 12:17.

Following the lies of false witnesses leads to disobedience. Many will choose and practice evil to bring harm. I pray this, my son, will not be your choice. Choose wisdom that is more than knowledge!

Finally, ask God for wisdom that brings understanding - wisdom is more than knowledge in all things. Through the wisdom of God, there is a set order of things. God systematically established our world. There is sunset and sunrise as part of God's order. The seasons of the year are a part of God's order. Rain and clouds are a part of God's order. With God's wisdom, you can operate in order and not operate out of season. That is what the men in our neighborhood understood in their journey.

As God said to the exiled in Jerusalem, "For I know the plans I have for you; plans to prosper you and not to harm you, plans to give you hope and a future. Then you will call on me and come and pray to me, and I will listen to you. You will seek me and find me when you seek me with all your heart. I will be found by you, and will bring you back from captivity," Jeremiah 29:11-14 NIV.

Prayer Thoughts

Jesus said, "Let the little children come to me, and do not hinder them, for the kingdom of God belongs to such as these. Truly I tell you, anyone who will not receive the kingdom of God like a little child will never enter it." And he took the children in his arms, placed his hands on them, and blessed them.

Dear God, Our Heavenly Father, Our Abba,

Thankful for the gift of children. We pray, in the name of Jesus Christ, that the blood of Jesus cover them now and forever. We declare by the authority that you have given us through Christ Jesus, that they have the mind of Christ. Your loving arms protect them from the arrows of the enemy. They are deflected and aimed at destroying the enemy. We declare that the blood of Jesus covers our children, youth, and young adults. They are covered in all areas of their lives. They succeed in the assignments and territories assigned to them by You. They are protected in the earthly realm, which includes justice, government, financial systems, educational systems, and social systems. We call forth the ministering angels, guardian angels, messengers of heaven, and even Gabriel fight on their behalf. Their spiritual growth is in Your mighty hands. Our children leap over walls in victory. They are more than conquerors. They are vessels of honor who serve you in Spirit and in Truth. They do not conform to this world; rather, they lay up their treasures in heaven. Your will concerning them is done.

We thank you for answering this prayer, in the name of Jesus.

Amen.

Chapter 12

Beautiful photo taken by my friend, Althea.

BITTERSWEET

One of the most challenging things to get over is judgmental calls. Yelp! Judgmental calls! Is there such a thing? Of course, there is! Let me explain my take on this and how it ties to the title "Bittersweet."

Take sports, for example. Watching as a spectator or from the sideline is easier than being in the game. The spectator's view is different from that of the referee and player. Personal biases, differences, short-sightedness, and obstruction may cloud spectators' views. At the same time, the referee's decision is tied to protocols or rules of the sport. The player's performance is connected to personal endurance, training, opposition, and team players. And at any time, a wrong decision could cost dreams and dreamers.

What's the price? First, "Do not sit out of the game for fear of mistakes – on your part or others?" Being involved in change can be beneficial. How so?

Well, as I see it, you can view decisions into two categories: (1) Man's Standards and (2) God's Standards. Man's standards change. God's standards do not. Man's standards are not always fair; they can be clouded by personal biases, personal favorites, and man's desire to control others' lives. God's standards do not change because He is the same today, yesterday, and will be so tomorrow.

Perhaps you know of a situation when a man's standards cost someone a game, a job, or another loss. I recall when the parents of "School A" and the school had high hopes for a playoff bid. That season, the School A team had only two losses. Unfortunately, to their surprise, they did not qualify for the playoffs based on the Association's standards. This was disheartening to all, especially to the coaches and team. They worked hard as competitors for a winning season and had a successful year in their conference. The decision to offer the bid to another group was a bittersweet moment.

Yet, it was essential to help the team see themselves still as a successful championship team by their own standards. It was essential to help them remember that they were internally built to weather victories and losses.

As a parent, it can be difficult to explain the decision-making process of others when your child is feeling hurt. People from all walks of life face this dreadful task of explaining/understanding bittersweet times. But bittersweet times can be a place of healing. God's testing ground so that you grow.

You might be the one who needs to encourage change in difficult times. Change can be difficult, but it can also lead to positive outcomes. It may require the champions/the team to ensure that things change for the better. Having conversations and taking positive steps is not just for emotional healing but a spiritual step in a difficult situation.

The image at the beginning of this chapter depicts a garden filled with many colorful flowers. While each one is different, together, they form a beautiful garden.

Unfortunately, not everyone will see the beauty of your garden – your team. They will pass up the opportunity to view the value of differences. They may refuse to allow additional *seeds* that have been proven to grow well in the garden. Some people may even prefer to destroy the garden rather than expand its potential to be a greater, more beautiful one. This is bittersweet.

What can anyone say when these things happen? Well, we might react with words, i.e., *"Tuck in your chin; things will get better. There is always next year."* The truth is that we might find ourselves in a similar situation next year, given the current human conditions. Still, we must bring hope with encouraging words for the bittersweet times. You may be the one who needs to lift someone's spirit in these times.

In these times, God's standards are most comforting to the team. God's standards build. God's standards are meant to move you forward for victory. God has said that you are to be an overcomer; overcomers go over walls, setting criteria for winning victories in and out of season.

That is why great coaches and teams return to the field; they come back to the battle with the mindset of winners. That is why determined parents continue to build up, rather than tear down, focusing on generational blessings and breaking down generational curses. That is why, even as players, you are not alone.

People will challenge winners. Winners are meant to be challenged fairly and unfairly. The race is given to those who will hold out. The

"Outstanding Leadership Award" goes to the teams/players that refuse to accept defeat based on man's standards. That is why they are comeback kids when people count champion teams out. "It is not what people say; it is what they believe. It is what you believe. So a man thinks that is the way he will go. For example, "If I believe that I am more than your standards, more than a conqueror, who can stop me?"

There is another scenario to bittersweet. You must not forget that victories can be bittersweet in the natural world. Why? Once you are seen as a winner, there is an expectation to be even greater. The spectators may turn against you even in victory. How often have people risen to the top of their game and walked away with bittersweet memories after a winning streak? One incident could cause that same cheering crowd to turn on you. Ask Jesus about that. That cheering crowd that honored him at his entry into Jerusalem was among those who shouted, "Crucify Him," a few days later. Therefore, how well do you handle the bittersweet time when the tides turn?

What is most important? Man's standards or God's standards? What will move you forward in victory? How you handle the situation is largely determined by your mindset.

Again, you have an opportunity to turn the bittersweet into a chance to showcase the traits of a winner – a champion! There is grace in winning and grace in losing for a comeback victory.

Spiritually, in bittersweet times, God's standards mean you are victorious. Your victory is assured when you stay on His team in life. This Coach does not tire. This Coach has the resources for the assignment. Yes, like David against Goliath, you always have the best coach with Him. You will view bittersweet times differently as a team player, both naturally and spiritually. The opportunities are more significant in turning things around in your favor. The off-seasons are no off-seasons. They are opportunities given by God for you to grow. They are opportunities to showcase His greatness.

Yes, His standards make the difference in bittersweet.

WHY SONS AND GRANDSONS?

YOU HAVE THE PROMISE OF A LEGACY THAT YOU DESERVE

God had a special plan from the beginning for Humanity – family and fellowship. From Adam, Noah, and Abraham, His plan continued through the work of Jesus Christ.

Man still has a choice to choose God. It is God's will that all be saved, but truly not everyone will be. Many will deny Jesus as Savior.

This book is written as an extension of support to a segment of believers, young males. They have the awesome task as young men of God to walk in faith among many who wish to see their demise. As prayer warriors, mothers, fathers, ministers, teachers, servant leaders, siblings, and fellow believers to come, it is our job to cover them, to watch, and to pray. The enemy (devil) understands that a man of faith walks in God's strength and character and that man is to be feared.

Recognizing that everyday living is a challenge, especially for young males, servant leaders must be vigilant in their calling to support them in every area of their lives for the glory of God. This will honor God. Contrary to what the enemy wants man to believe, there are more blessings than challenges. God is the Sustainer of good.

Quite often, I hear from others, including mentors, about their desire to support young males in their faith walk. Like them, I am aware of some of the battles that they face. It is my sincere hope that this book conveys a message of hope for sons and grandsons. I pray that this book blesses those who share it, read it, and view what God has in store for each of us. I pray *for watchmen in the city who will guard this special assignment concerning this generation* as they travail in faith. We are not defenseless, but we must be about God's agenda in our warring, interceding for these young soldiers. God holds all of His children accountable as faithful and loving members of the same household. As members of the same body, we must amplify His love by caring and serving. We must let them know that they are not alone in their fight for a purposeful life in Him.

Hopefully, you will find words in this book that mirror those teachings as mothers, grandmothers, fathers, grandfathers, guardians, and guardian angels. It is our intent to support the young men in the legacy that God wants them to have - a legacy that mirrors the Father for impact.

You never know who will touch your life. Thank God for the many spiritual fathers and mothers in our lives.

Do not forget the trailblazers in your life – honor spiritual landmarks!

ABOUT THE AUTHOR & RELATED BOOKS

Rev. Dr. Gardenia T. Bulluck is a wife, mother, grandmother, writer, retired public school educator, Christian Educator, and ordained minister. She holds a Doctorate of Ministry degree from Northwestern Theological Seminary in New Port Richey, Florida. She received her Master's and Specialist Degrees in Education from Barry University of Miami, Florida, and a business degree from Shaw University, Raleigh, North Carolina.

As a retired educator, she has credentials that include certification as a public-school teacher and in school administration. For decades, she has worked with diverse populations, including students with special needs and English language learners (ELL). She continues to have a high interest in academics and community development. She has been an entrepreneur in the non-profit sector, working with families and children to improve literacy. She established a non-profit organization to provide health and academic support, aiming to reduce the number of children lacking the necessary skill sets to succeed academically, decrease delinquent behavior in youth due to a lack of basic necessities, and prevent malnutrition in children. The program expanded with a knowledgeable management team to assist children and families in meeting their basic needs, such as shelter, food, and clothing, while providing information and resources to help them move towards self-sustainability.

website: bulluckg.com.

www.ingramcontent.com/pod-product-compliance
Lightning Source LLC
Chambersburg PA
CBHW081253040426
42453CB00014B/2400